For Lindsey. See you soon.

MIDNIGHT

ABIGAIL DE NIVERVILLE

Copyright © 2021 Abigail de Niverville

All rights reserved. No part of this book may be reproduced, performed, or used in any manner whatsoever without written consent from the author, except in reviews where brief quotations are permitted.

Website: adeniverville.com

Twitter/Facebook: @adeniverville

Cover Photo and Design: Cristina Nikolic of NXSTY MEDIA

Formatting: Ceillie Simkiss

MIDNIGHT

In that liminal space
between asleep and awake
everything
comes to light.

ON THE BUSIEST STREET

Last night
the birds sang from my window
on the busiest street
in a city that never sleeps
and in the midst of all this unease
I loved it.

DANDELION GIRL

You are gentle sunshine,
the food for bees
before the beautiful flowers bloom.
You are beautiful too,
born to endure this harsh world,
choking out those around you.

You don't choke because you long to be cruel
you choke because you long to be free
and beauty often has its thorns
and convention often makes no difference.

Dandelion girl
though cut down over again
you flourish—
roots strong enough to last decades
powerful enough to regrow.

There are many
who seek out dandelion girls

to pull them from the soil
as a challenge.

Though uprooted
you grow back
with venom.

DON'T LOOK BACK IN ANGER

Do flowers still grow
in gardens left behind?
Or was I the force
keeping them alive?

HEALING

I wonder
if I can begin
if I have it inside
to write without pain—
without words
pulling out a knife.

HERITAGE

I don't know how
to explain.

Like many
I am countries
upon countries
stacked together,
split apart,
displaced.

Grandpa was Jewish—
I still hear the word
spat in my face.

Still feel the ache
of a family tree
with missing names.

I wish I knew
how to explain.

Turn to the mirror:
so unlike
what stared back at me
when I was a little girl
and "Jewish"
meant "ugly."

Can you let me off the hook
and forgive for me?

It's too much,
this weight,
I'm sorry.

MARY JANES IN THE FIREPLACE

A child once lived here
you know
I know—
did she follow you home?

Or was she waiting
for someone
to be listening?

TO HILDEGARDE OF BINGEN

Did you really get divine inspiration?
Or did no one believe
a woman could be amazing?

MARY MAGDALENE

I won't say
I think
they were married
but I often wonder
what if they'd been.

What would it mean
to love a man
so devoted to one cause
one goal
one purpose?

Did she believe it?
Did he?
Would he whisper
secrets in the night
of a future
that could never be?

I wonder
if she tried

to paint his face in her heart
if she saw beyond
God and prophecy.

I wonder
what her dreams had been
before the world shifted
cast her out
labeled her worthless.

I wonder how she
first felt that call
when she caught
the words of the prophet.
Did she run towards the sound?
Or did it run towards her?

How did it begin?
A glance across a room
like the stories of old?
A meeting of eyes
the slight touching of hands?

What did it mean?
Fire
rain
starlight
lightning?

Did he love her the way
some tell us to love a woman?
He must have known
there were other ways.

Touch is not essential

to find
a heart beating
a pulse racing.

He may have loved her
with his whole soul
shared every fear
and hope
and desire
and in turn
she gave them
so freely.

That's a man
worth mourning
for eternity.

UNTOLD STORIES

At the gallery I read about
Riopelle and Mitchell:
their relationship
so sweet
yet undefined.
Never once
did the panels express
exactly what they were
to each other.

Did they ever
whisper it
or did they simply exist
in a strange limbo
of unspoken feelings
expectations
desires
as so many of us have?

The colours on canvas—
what did they express?

Hidden meanings
or nothingness?

In the end
he left her
for a younger artist
at a retreat she'd hosted—
the same roof
that once carried their love.

What does it carry
now that they're ghosts?

Green:
the colour of healing
endurance
harmony
self-respect
fertility
balance
rest.

Let me heal
this weary mind
endure the coldest nights
like the rock
I so long to be.

Paint
my whole life green
just so it means
I'll grow into the person
I've always dreamed:

a statue
with moss for hair
and fingerprints
over my heart.

DEAR AMANDA LOVELACE

I read
about the princess
who became
the hero she needed

But I can't
I can't
I can't.

CROCUSES

Crocus blooms remind me
of a brown house
a back porch
and mint green carpet.

The corner cabinet
white figurines
of Jesus and Mary.

Brown recliner in the dining room,
tapestry of a woman dancing,
a hidden cabinet with screech,
and everything in between.

My cousin in the dunes
painted by my mother,
an old relative in army regalia
that no one remembers,
the card shuffling machine
my dad hated—
all together

somehow
they became connected.

Every Easter
when the crocus blooms,
I see it in the front yard
of this brown house—
reminds me of my Nanna's arms
my aunt K's wit
and the dress-up clothes
stuffed in the closet.

Hey Mom,
how are you?
Have the flowers grown?

Hey Mom,
I miss you—
when am I coming home?

1997—
when Sarah
planted forget-me-nots,
I bet
no one thought
they'd mean so much.

The backyard
has grown wild
with them.

See you soon.

CAPITALISM

We've come to a point
where even sleeping
is an act
of rebellion.

ENDING

How it feels
when the war is over:

MUSEUM

I remember
the quiet
open place

Do you?

I remember
the printed
name plates

Do you?

I remember
wandering aimlessly,
no purpose,
all vacancies,
absorbing useless information
that made me better
somehow,
taking pictures
of names and places

—to research later
(and then don't)

And
breathing.

I remember
breathing

Do you?

———

Your face
in all my dreams
in all my nightmares.

I'm not scared
anymore.

I don't know
if I feel happiness
or hatred
when I look at you.

The lines between both
have become
so undefined.

Your eyes
are nothing like the sun—
your lips, red:
exactly
like the demon he described.

It's easier to see you
as a demon in my mind.

ELEVEN

I was eleven
saw myself as grown
the world was opening
and I
was making changes for it.

Now I see
eleven
too young:
I don't want
to grow
for anyone.

SEVENTEEN

They say the theatre
is for the misfits
the unwanted
unconventional
ugly
cast out by society.

I never had my chance
to be the princess.

*What does that
make me?*

TWENTY

The clock was ticking.

Time is running out
to have everything.

Wish I could hold me in my arms and say
"it's okay
to be left waiting."

HOPE

If cities didn't separate
where would we be?

I'm afraid to wonder—
haven't hoped
in centuries.

HEART

A church with no walls
nor roof
is still a sanctuary.

I wish the rain would come
and show you
how much it loves you.

That's what they say
the flowers
and the rain
two halves of a whole
together again.

HOME

I long to feel
the tide
rising and falling
over my body.
Standing tall
like a rock carved
from the landscape—
belonging.

In some ways
I have never belonged there—
nor believed
a man could save me
or a baby at nineteen
was old enough
or the city
would kill me.

FROM THE WINDOW

A purple streak
against a grey strip
two white orbs
pulsing beneath it

(the bus
is early)

I measure time spent
in books I've read:
seven this month.

Feels so long
since that first book
even longer
since the last.

When I think about time
without books
it passes too fast
but when I think in seven books
time is
infinite.

SCREEN LIFE

I'm out there—
do you care?

DEPRESSION, PT. 2

The doctor is out—
don't come looking for me.
I need to find
my missing piece.

The arrival of weekly flyers
brings joy never understood
until
standing in this empty room
full of desperation and hopes
and possibilities—
for once
having the means
to make this empty
my home.

DEEP THOUGHTS

Whatever happened
to show
not tell?

It
died.

FRENCH ON THE BRAIN

It's time
to close the lights.

Dual languages
cloud my mind.

11:11

Make a wish…

Beautiful
darling
dearest.

MIDNIGHT, PT 2

Magic occurs
in the purple darkness.
Stay awake,
see what happens—
until violet
becomes black behind eyelids,
the pull of nighttime descends,
pressing fingers onto skin,
whispering
wait
to wake up
and do it again.

And in the space
between dreaming and awake
there's nothing
but me.

And in the time
between truth and lie
there's nothing
but me.

Nothing but the quiet
and me.

ACKNOWLEDGMENTS

A huge thank you to early beta readers of this collection, who gave me the encouragement to pursue working towards publishing it. Big thank you to Ael, Jacquie, Bridget, and Mara. You're all stars.

Thank you to Shelby Eileen for editing an earlier version of this manuscript and providing vital feedback in improving it. I have so much respect for your work, and I'm grateful for your input.

Thank you to Ceillie Simkiss for formatting the book and being a generally great friend in the writing trenches.

And finally, a thank you to Cristina Nikolic, for the amazing cover and moral support.

Abigail de Niverville is an author, composer, and poet based in Toronto, Canada. Born on the East Coast, Abigail draws inspiration from her experiences growing up there. When she's not writing words frantically, she composes music and holds an M.Mus from the University of Toronto. Her debut novel *I Knew Him* was released in 2019 by NineStar Press and is available through most major book retailers. Her second novel *We Go Together* was published by NineStar Press in 2020.

If you liked this collection of poems, stay up to date with Abigail's future releases by signing up for her newsletter at https://adeniverville.com/.

www.ingramcontent.com/pod-product-compliance
Lightning Source LLC
Chambersburg PA
CBHW051815050726
47598CB00006B/2574